FAMOUS CAMPAIGNERS FOR CHANGE

Nina Morgan

Wayland

Famous people

Famous Artists
Famous Campaigners for Change
Famous Explorers
Famous Inventors
Famous Musicians
Famous Scientists

Picture acknowledgements

Camera Press/SK Dutt 21, 22, 23; Mary Evans 12, 14 (lower), 16; Eye Ubiquitous/
PM Field 20,/Julia Waterlow 35; Peter Newark 4 (lower), 5, 6, 7, 8, 9, 30, 31;
Popperfoto 14 (top), 15, 17, 18, 19, 27, 28, 29, 32, 33, 36 (top), 38, 42, 43, 44; Rex
Features/Dieter Ludwig 24; Mark Edwards/Still Pictures 39, 40, Edward Parker/
Still Pictures 41; Topham 4 (top), 13, 25, 26, 34/Alison Wright, 36 (lower), 45;
Wayland Picture Library 10, 11, 19/Tim Woodcock.
Cover artwork by Peter Dennis.

Series editor: Rosemary Ashley
Series designer: Malcolm Walker

First published in 1993 by
Wayland (Publishers) Limited
61 Western Road, Hove
East Sussex, BN3 1JD, England

British Library Cataloguing in Publication Data
Morgan, Nina
    Famous Campaigners for Change. -(Famous People Series)
    I. Title II. Series
    322.4092

ISBN 0-7502-0667-5

Typeset by Kudos Editorial and Design Services
Printed and bound in Italy by Rotolito Lombardo S.p.A, Milan

Contents

Frederick Douglass
The slave who fought for equal rights 4

Florence Nightingale
The founder of modern nursing 8

Mohandas Gandhi
The prophet of non-violence 12

Maria Montessori
The teacher who changed the face of schools 16

Mother Teresa
'Something beautiful for God' 20

Nelson Mandela
Champion of black South Africans 25

Martin Luther King
'I have a dream' 29

The Dalai Lama
Patient worker for world peace 34

Chico Mendes
Fighting to save the rainforest 38

Aung San Suu Kyi
'A bright collection of strange victories' 42

Glossary 46
Books to read and further information 47
Index 48

Introduction

What sort of person becomes a campaigner for change?
This is how the poet Wordsworth described such a person:

*One in who persuasion and belief
Had ripened into faith, and faith become
A passionate intuition.*

Here are the stories of ten men and women who all developed a 'passionate intuition' that convinced them they must campaign for change in some aspect of life. Each has tried to bring about change by peaceful methods, and in their various ways and for their various causes, all have devoted their lives to trying to make the world a better place for all people everywhere.

Frederick *Douglass*

The slave who fought for equal rights

Frederick Douglass was born on a slave plantation. He taught himself to read and write, and when he was twenty-one he escaped to the North. He worked hard to end slavery and became one of the most important human rights leaders of the nineteenth century.

A poster advertising the sale of slaves. Until the end of the Civil War in 1865, black people were sold as slaves to work in the fields of the southern United States.

Frederick Douglass was born into slavery in Maryland in the southern United States in 1818 but he ended his life as a free man, living in the North. His mother was a black slave. His father, who he never knew, was white. When he was only eight years old Frederick was taken from his mother and sent to be a house slave in the city of Baltimore. Later he returned to work on the plantation where he had been born.

VALUABLE GANG OF YOUNG NEGROES

By JOS. A. BEARD.

Will be sold at Auction,

ON WEDNESDAY, 25TH INST.

At 12 o'clock, at Banks' Arcade,

17 Valuable Young Negroes, Men and Women, Field Hands. Sold for no fault; with the best city guarantees.

Sale Positive and without reserve!

☞**TERMS CASH.**

New Orleans, March 24, 1840.

Slaves were forced to work long hours in the fields. If they did not work hard enough, their owners would beat them.

Education was forbidden to slaves, so Frederick secretly taught himself to read and write. Throughout his life, he longed to be free, and when he was twenty-one he escaped to the North, where it was against the law to keep slaves. He escaped along the 'underground railroad', an escape route organized by people who were against slavery and wanted to help those who were fleeing from it.

Once he reached the North, Frederick Douglass settled in Boston, Massachusetts. There he joined the abolitionists, a group of people who wanted to bring slavery to an end. He also wrote a book called *Narrative of the Life of Frederick Douglass, An American Slave*. In the book he described the beatings and cruelty he had suffered at the hands of his owners. For many people this book provided their first glimpse of what slavery actually meant. When they realized what a cruel system it was they became determined to join the

A photograph showing slaves on a sugar cane plantation. Crops of sugar cane, tobacco and cotton brought great wealth to the plantation owners while the slaves lived in poverty.

Slaves photographed planting sweet potatoes in 1860. In 1865 the Civil War ended in victory for the North and slavery became illegal all over the United States.

Dates

1818 born in Maryland, USA
1838 escapes along the 'underground railroad' to the North
1841 joins the abolitionist movement
1845 writes *Narrative of the Life of Frederick Douglass, An American Slave*; travels to Britain and Ireland.
1847 returns to the USA and publishes the *North Star*
1861-65 American Civil War; becomes an adviser to President Lincoln
1871-1886 holds various government jobs
1889-92 serves as US government minister and consul-general to Haiti
1895 dies

growing band of abolitionists. To avoid recapture by his owner, Douglass left America after writing his book, to spend two years lecturing in Britain and Ireland.

When he returned to the United States in 1847, Douglass founded a newspaper, the *North Star*, which pressed for the abolition of slavery. Douglass' work helped to persuade President Abraham Lincoln that slavery must be ended. When the American Civil War broke out in 1861, Douglass became an adviser to the President. He also persuaded many black volunteers to join the northern army and fight against slavery alongside white soldiers.

Although the Civil War ended in victory for the North in 1865, and slavery was made illegal throughout the United States, Douglass realized that there were still many battles to be fought before all people could be equal. He worked in various government jobs and continued to strive for freedom for all people until his death in 1895.

Florence Nightingale

The founder of modern nursing

Florence Nightingale wanted to improve conditions for sick people. Hospitals, when she was young, were dirty and crowded and nurses were often rough and uncaring. When she was asked to care for wounded soldiers fighting in the Crimean War, she immediately set to work to improve the terrible conditions she found there. Back in London she founded the first training school for nurses. Her work in training nurses and improving hospital conditions means that her name will never be forgotten.

Florence Nightingale was born on 12 May 1820 in the city of Florence in Italy. Her wealthy parents hoped that she would follow the path of most upper-class English girls and spend her time visiting friends and going to parties, in the hope of meeting a wealthy husband. But Florence had other ideas.

Florence Nightingale (seated) with her sister Parthenope. Their wealthy parents hoped that both their daughters would settle down as housewives and mothers.

When she was eighteen, Florence became convinced that God had a purpose for her – to care for the sick. This idea horrified her parents, because in those days nurses were usually rough women, with little or no medical training. But in spite of her parents' objections, Florence secretly studied nursing and worked out plans for improving the running of hospitals. Gradually she overcame her parents' opposition, and began visiting and working in hospitals.

In 1854 Florence Nightingale was asked to lead a group of nurses to care for British soldiers wounded in the bloody battles of the Crimean War. In this war French and British soldiers were fighting and dying alongside Turkish soldiers, to keep the Russians out of the Crimea – a piece of land that sticks out into the Black Sea.

When she arrived with her nurses, Florence Nightingale found thousands of sick and wounded British soldiers crammed into a filthy hospital with not enough food and supplies. Within a few weeks she had arranged for the hospital to be cleaned and had organized food and medical supplies.

A photograph taken of Florence Nightingale when she was in her thirties.

When Florence arrived with her nurses at the army hospital at Scutari in Turkey, one of her first tasks was to clean and organize the filthy wards.

As a result, the sick and wounded were far more comfortable. She was devoted to the care of her patients and the soldiers loved her. They called her the 'Lady of the Lamp' because each night she walked through the dark wards with her lamp, bringing comfort to the sick and dying.

Florence Nightingale returned home in 1856 and was hailed as a heroine. But she took no notice of all the praise and instead set about working to improve army hospitals in England. She also concerned herself with health problems in British colonies overseas, especially India.

Florence Nightingale became a well-known adviser on nursing all over the world. In 1860 she established the first training school for nurses, the Nightingale School for Nurses at St Thomas's Hospital in London. She did not teach at the school, but instead organized the training and provided much advice. She laid down strict rules for the behaviour of nurses and made sure they were taught basic skills of first aid and hygiene. The nurses were also taught to run hospital wards in an organized and orderly way. Many of them went on to work abroad and brought her ideas to other countries; her methods form the basis of nursing training today.

In 1907 Florence Nightingale was awarded the Order of Merit by King Edward VII. This was the first time that this great honour had ever been given to a woman. After a long life of service to other people, she died in 1910, at the age of ninety.

Dates

1820 born in Florence, Italy
1838 becomes convinced that she should devote her life to the care of the sick and poor
1853-56 The Crimean War
1854 leads a group of nurses to look after British soldiers in the army hospital in Scutari in Turkey
1860 sets up the first training school for nurses at St Thomas's Hospital, London
1907 awarded the Order of Merit
1910 dies in London at the age of ninety

A photograph of Florence Nightingale with some of the newly-trained Nightingale nurses at St Thomas' Hospital.

Mohandas *Gandhi*

The prophet of non-violence

Mohandas Gandhi fought against injustice all his life. He led his people in peaceful protest to bring about change. His ideas of non-violent protest earned him great respect for his courage and his principles. Workers for peace and campaigners for change all around the world still follow his example.

Mohandas Gandhi, nicknamed Mahatma (or Great Soul), worked throughout his life for equal rights for the Indian people. He helped to lead his country to independence from the British, who ruled India.

Gandhi was born on 2 October 1869, in the city of Porbandar in western India. Although he was never a brilliant student at school, he was admitted to the University of Bombay when he was eighteen years old. A year later he sailed for England to study law.

Life was difficult for the young Indian in London, but he passed his examinations. After returning to India he went to work as a lawyer in South Africa.

Gandhi was amazed to find how unfairly Indians and blacks were treated in South Africa. In 1906, when the South African government introduced a law requiring Indians to carry registration certificates, which identified them as Indians and foreigners, his patience snapped. He urged his fellow Indians to protest against the law by simply not registering and to calmly accept the punishment for their actions. This was the first of many protests that Gandhi organized throughout his life, based on his principle of peaceful protest or passive resistance.

Throughout his life Gandhi was inspired by his belief in *satyagraha*, the truth force. He believed passionately in the use of non-violent, or passive resistance, to fight injustice.

Gandhi always wore his simple loincloth and shawl, even when visiting the British Prime Minister, at Downing Street in London.

(left) Gandhi lived simply all his life. He learnt to spin because he believed Indian people should make things, such as thread for weaving, rather than buy them.

Women carrying banners through the streets of Bombay in 1930, in protest against unjust British laws.

In 1930 Gandhi broke the law to protest against an unfair tax on salt. He and his followers walked to the coast to collect their own salt.

When a law was unjust, Gandhi urged his followers to calmly refuse to cooperate, and then quietly accept the punishment for their actions. When huge numbers of people followed this advice, the results were astonishing.

In 1915 Gandhi returned to India. Like many others he longed to see his country free from British rule. In 1919 he led a campaign for self-rule, calling for peaceful protest against the British authorities. When he organized a one-day general strike throughout India he was horrified at the violence this action unleashed. He was arrested and sentenced to six years in prison for his part in organizing the strike.

After his release from prison, Gandhi continued to organize a series of non-violent protests, even though his actions meant that he spent

many more years in prison. But he never gave up the struggle. Finally, on 15 August 1947, India was granted independence from Britain.

After independence there was terrible fighting between the Hindu and Muslim populations. To try to stop the fighting Gandhi began a fast as he had done many times before. This was his way of protesting against the violence and this time he was prepared to die. His action worked and the fighting soon stopped. But not everyone was satisfied. On 30 January 1948, Gandhi went to a prayer meeting. A Hindu man, angry because he felt Gandhi was not doing enough for Hindus, suddenly broke from the crowd and shot him. Gandhi died almost at once.

The Prime Minister of the new India broke the sad news to the nation, saying 'The light has gone out of our lives.' But the ideas of peaceful protest developed by the man who worked 'for the brotherhood of man under the fatherhood of God', live on in the hearts of many people all over the world.

Dates

1869 born at Porbandar in western India
1887 travels to England to study law
1893 goes to South Africa to work; looks after the interests of Indians in South Africa
1906 organizes peaceful protest against registration law
1915 returns to India
1919 organizes non-violent resistance against the British and calls a general strike to protest for self-rule for India; sent to prison for six years
1930 organizes protests against tax on salt
1942 imprisoned after campaign of passive resistance but is involved in discussions for independence
1947 India granted independence
1948 assassinated

Mohandas Gandhi with his grand-daughters, who looked after him until the end of his life.

Maria *Montessori*

The teacher who changed the face of schools

Schools in the early twentieth century were strict and not much fun, because teachers thought that children would only learn if they were forced to do so. Maria Montessori did not agree. She opened a school with bright classrooms and plenty of well-made toys and games. Because of her work, most schools are pleasanter places than they used to be.

Maria Montessori believed that all children are eager to learn if they are given the right environment. Because of her ideas, today's schools are bright, cheerful and inviting places in which to learn.

Maria was born on 31 August 1870 in Chiaraville, Italy. She studied medicine at the University of Rome and in 1896 she became the first woman in Italy to receive a degree in medicine. After gaining her degree she worked with children with learning disabilities. She became convinced that if they were given the right surroundings and equipment, these children could learn more than anyone ever expected.

A small boy at school in 1937. He is learning to concentrate and to count, using the Montessori method.

As a result of her findings, Maria Montessori founded a school in Rome where children with learning disabilities could study. She provided the children with bright, comfortable and welcoming classrooms, and encouraged them to learn at their own pace, using colourful, attractive equipment. The results were remarkable – many children who were believed to be unteachable did learn and were given a chance to grow up to have independent lives.

Maria Montessori realized that if her methods worked for children with learning disabilities, the results might be even more dramatic with children who did not have such problems. To find out, she set up a *Casa dei Bambini* or Children's House, in the slums of Rome. To everyone's surprise, the ragged and unruly slum children came to the *Casa* because they enjoyed being there. They were soon transformed into well-behaved and obedient pupils who were eager to learn. Many of the children in the *Casa* learned to read and write before they were five.

(opposite) Children in a Montessori school in 1915, using toys and games to help them learn.

After the success of her first *Casa dei Bambini*, Maria Montessori went on to set up schools based on her methods throughout Italy and in many other countries. She also set up a network of training schools to teach her educational ideas to teachers.

The Montessori method encourages children to learn by providing them with an environment suitable for their age and stage of development. The children learn at their own

Maria Montessori saw her methods working at first hand on a visit to a London school in 1951.

pace, working with well-designed games and equipment. By making schools pleasant and interesting places in which to study, the Montessori method helps children to learn self-discipline and self-confidence, along with the basic skills of reading, writing and arithmetic.

Today's bright classrooms owe much to the influence of Maria Montessori.

Maria Montessori left Italy in 1934, because she did not agree with the government of the time. She continued to travel, setting up training schools and explaining her methods until her death in The Netherlands, at the age of eighty-two.

Although not everyone agrees with all aspects of the Montessori method, the ideas of Maria Montessori are the influence behind the bright classrooms, child-sized furniture, educational games and many of the teaching methods that are used in all types of schools today.

Dates

1870 birth in Chiaraville, Italy
1896 gains a degree in medicine
1907 opens her first *Casa dei Bambini* in the slums of Rome
1934 leaves Italy, but continues to set up Montessori schools throughout the world
1952 dies in The Netherlands

Mother *Teresa*

'Something beautiful for God'

Mother Teresa devotes her life to serving the poor and the sick. In 1946 she heard a call from God, telling her to go out into the streets and care for the homeless and sick people of Calcutta. From small beginnings she has built up a religious organization, The Missionaries of Charity, who bring care and love to the 'poorest of the poor' throughout the world.

In 1946, a Catholic nun teaching in a girls' school in Calcutta, India heard a call from God, telling her to go and serve amongst the 'poorest of the poor'. Today Mother Teresa heads a world-wide religious organization dedicated to serving the poor. She preaches a message of hope, love and dignity to all people everywhere.

On 27 August 1910 Agnes Gonxha Bojaxhiu was born in Skopje, Macedonia, into an Albanian Catholic family. By the time she was twelve years old, the young Agnes knew that God had a plan for her life; she would beome a missionary nun.

Thousands of people live in makeshift shacks or on the bare streets of Calcutta.

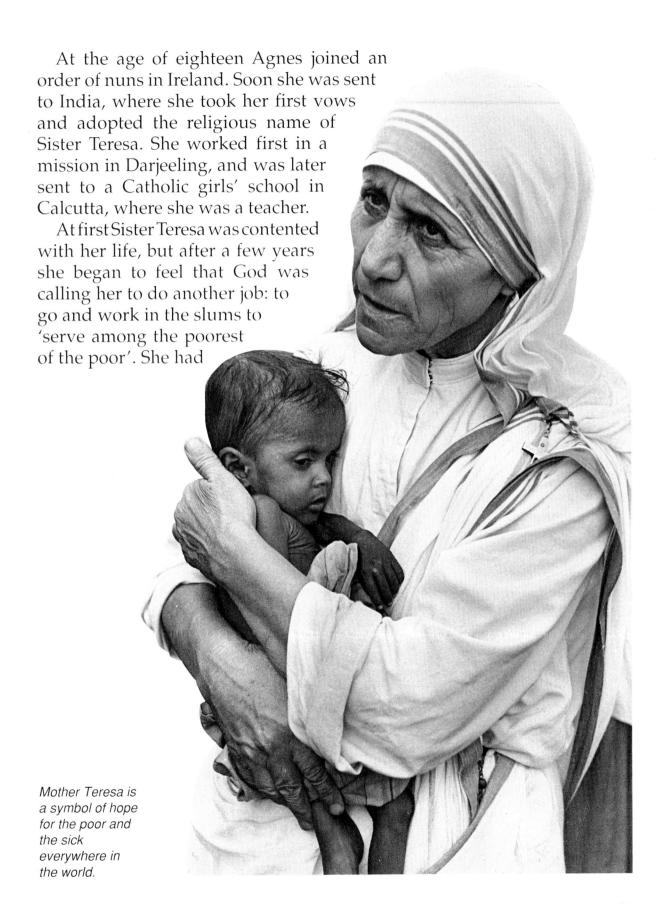

At the age of eighteen Agnes joined an order of nuns in Ireland. Soon she was sent to India, where she took her first vows and adopted the religious name of Sister Teresa. She worked first in a mission in Darjeeling, and was later sent to a Catholic girls' school in Calcutta, where she was a teacher.

At first Sister Teresa was contented with her life, but after a few years she began to feel that God was calling her to do another job: to go and work in the slums to 'serve among the poorest of the poor'. She had

Mother Teresa is a symbol of hope for the poor and the sick everywhere in the world.

a difficult task persuading the church authorities to allow her to go out into the Calcutta streets to work among the poor.

While she waited for permission from the Church, she took a course in first aid and worked in a medical mission so that she would have some knowledge of caring for the sick. She also learnt the local language, Bengali. Finally, in 1950, Pope Pius XII allowed her to found a religious group, The Missionaries of Charity.

The missionaries started simply, running a small school and distributing food and medicines where they were most needed. As their numbers grew they opened homes for the poor and homeless people of Calcutta. They now devote themselves to working wholeheartedly among the poor of all religions. They distribute food and medicines and run homes

Missionaries of Charity distribute pills and medicines at a street clinic for the sick and homeless of Calcutta.

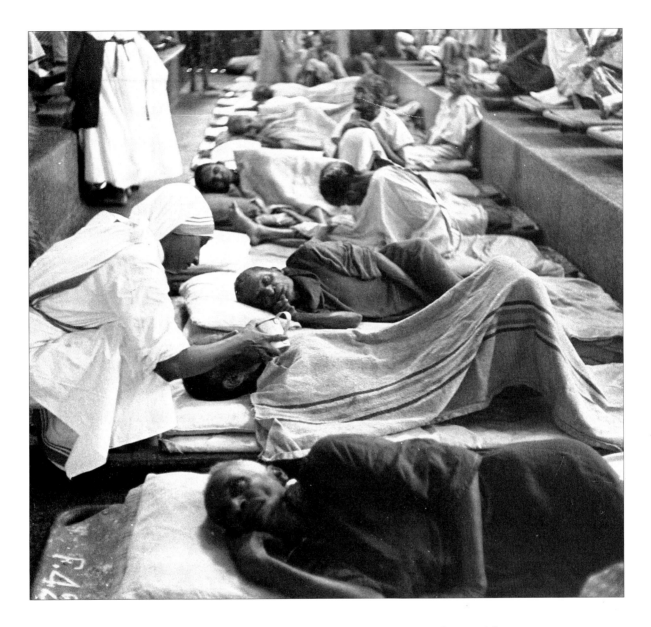

for the sick and the dying, where the poor can die with dignity. They also run homes for abandoned children, and clinics and shelters for lepers.

In 1963 a group of Missionary Brothers was set up to work alongside the nuns and two years later the Missionaries were told they could work wherever they were invited throughout the world. Mother Teresa has always said 'God will provide', and she has been proved right. Thousands of nuns and monks have joined, and from its small beginnings, the Missionaries of Charity now provide practical help and comfort for poor people all over the world.

This ward at Mother Teresa's Home for Dying Destitutes provides shelter and a place where people can die in dignity.

Mother Teresa and her Missionaries of Charity work to help people all over the world.

Mother Teresa has been awarded many prizes for her work, including the Nobel Peace Prize in 1979. She accepts these prizes not for herself, but for the people she serves. She and her Missionaries of Charity continue with their work, doing 'something beautiful for God', and persuading people to share and 'to love until it hurts'. She says; 'Let us always meet each other with a smile, for a smile is the beginning of love'.

Dates

1910 Agnes Gonxha Bojaxhiu born in Skopje, Macedonia
1928 joins a convent in Ireland and from there goes to a mission in Darjeeling, India
1928-48 teaches at St Mary's High School in Calcutta
1946 hears a call from God to go and work in the slums
1948 granted permission to leave the convent and work in the slums of Calcutta
1950 founds the Congregation of the Missionaries of Charity
1963 sets up associated group of Missionary brothers
1965 work of Missionaries of Charity begins outside India and spreads all over the world
1979 awarded Nobel Peace Prize

Nelson *Mandela*

Champion of black South Africans

Ever since he was a young man Nelson Mandela has worked to bring about a better life for black people in South Africa. After twenty-seven years in prison, he is free again to continue the struggle for a better life for black South Africans.

Nelson Mandela spent twenty-seven years in prison for his beliefs. He was freed in 1990 and is now serving as the President of the African National Congress (ANC), continuing his campaign for equality for black people in South Africa.

Mandela was born on 18 July 1918 in Qunu,

Nelson Mandela in 1960. In the following year he was forbidden to attend public meetings or leave Johannesburg, where he lived, because of his anti-apartheid activities.

a small tribal village in the Transkei region of South Africa. His parents gave him the name Rolihlahla, which means 'stirring up trouble' in his native language, Xhosa. This name proved to be a good description of the man Nelson Mandela was to become.

In 1940, Mandela travelled to the city of Johannesburg to study law. In the city he soon became aware of how unfairly black people were treated and decided to work to try to bring about change. He joined the African National Congress (ANC) in 1944, when he was a young law student, and he soon became an important member of the organization.

Mandela was born in this small tribal village in the Transkei region of South Africa.

The African National Congress was established in 1912 to unite Africans of different tribes, languages, religions and homelands, to fight for equal rights and to try to end the policy of apartheid in South Africa. Under apartheid laws

After his release from prison in 1990, Nelson Mandela became the leader of the African National Congress.

people were separated into groups on the basis of their colour and white people were considered to be superior.

In 1956, along with 154 other anti-apartheid campaigners, Mandela was charged with the crime of treason. After a trial which lasted for four years, all the campaigners were found not guilty. In 1960 the ANC was banned by the South African government and, because of his anti-apartheid activities, Mandela was forbidden to attend public meetings or to leave Johannesburg. But in spite of these orders, he continued to work secretly for the ANC. In 1962 he was arrested by the

Mandela meets South African President F.W. de Klerk. De Klerk has promised to try to bring about a fairer life for black people in South Africa.

South African authorities and two years later he was tried and sentenced to life imprisonment.

During his long years in prison Mandela received many international awards for his work to end apartheid, and human rights groups all over the world called for his release.

When he was finally set free on 11 February 1990, Nelson Mandela declared: 'today the majority of South Africans, black and white, recognize that apartheid has no future'. Now, thanks to the work of the ANC and other anti-apartheid organizations, attitudes in South Africa are changing. South African President F.W. de Klerk is trying to work with the ANC and other groups to bring about a fairer and better life for all South Africans, but there is still a long way to go.

Dates

1918 born in Qunu in the Transkei region of South Africa
1940 goes to Johannesburg to study law
1944 joins the African National Congress
1956 arrested with 154 others and accused of treason
1960 found not guilty of treason
1962 arrested and sentenced to five years hard labour
1964 sentenced to life imprisonment for offences related to ANC activities
1990 released from prison

Martin Luther *King*

'I have a dream'

Martin Luther King grew up in the southern United States. He saw how badly black people were treated and learned about the unfair laws that forced them to live separate lives from white people. He grew up to become a great leader in the movement for American civil rights. He died for his dream – which was that there should be equal rights for all people.

Martin Luther King was born on 15 January 1929 in Atlanta, Georgia in the southern United States. As a young boy, he was very unhappy to discover that he could not go to the same school as his white neighbours. He was also deeply hurt when he saw how badly

Martin Luther King was a powerful speaker, calling passionately for equal rights for all people.

Ramshackle cafés, serving blacks only, were once a common sight in the southern United States. Before the 1960s, many ordinary cafés and restaurants refused to serve black people.

his father, a minister in the Baptist Church, was treated by many white people. Martin grew up determined to make the South a fairer place for black people to live in.

Black people originally came from Africa to America to work as slaves in the huge plantations in the South. Although the slaves were officially freed in 1865, after the defeat of the Southern army in the American Civil War, black people continued to be treated as second-class citizens by many white southerners. Segregation laws were passed, to prevent blacks from mixing with whites; black children were forced to attend separate schools; black passengers had to ride separately from white passengers in buses, and many restaurants refused to serve black people.

When he was nineteen, Martin Luther King went to Boston, Massachusetts, to study to become a minister of religion.

Here, in the North, he found there was more freedom for black people. Six years later he returned to the South, to take up his work as a Baptist minister.

On his return he soon became involved with the struggle for equal rights for black people. When a black woman in Montgomery, Alabama, was arrested for refusing to give up her seat in a bus to a white passenger, King organized a boycott of the city buses, to try to force the authorities to give black people the same rights on buses as white people.

Black parents and children joined in peaceful demonstrations all over the South during the 1960s, to protest against segregation in schools.

In 1965 Martin Luther King led more than 10,000 people on a civil rights march. They walked more than eighty kilometres through the state of Alabama to demonstrate their belief in equal rights for all.

By 1959 King had become so involved in the struggle for equal rights that he left his church work to concentrate full time on the civil rights movement. In 1960 he joined black students in sit-ins at lunch counters (cafés), as they protested to try to end segregation in restaurants. He also joined the 'Freedom Riders', a group of black students who travelled on public buses throughout the South, demonstrating for equal rights for black people. He continued organizing non-violent demonstrations in the South, and in 1963 he led thousands of protestors, black and white, in a march to the US capital, Washington, where he spoke passionately about civil rights. 'I have a dream', he said, 'that my four little children will be judged not by the colour of their skin, but by the content of their character'.

Martin Luther King was a lifelong admirer of Mahatma Gandhi, and his ideas about the use of peaceful protest to bring about change. He urged his fellow blacks to use non-violent methods to bring about changes in the law. In l964 he was awarded the Nobel Peace Prize for his work for civil rights.

On 4 April 1968, King was shot dead by a white man, James Earl Ray, as he prepared to march with black workers in Memphis, Tennessee.

Thanks to Martin Luther King and other civil rights campaigners, segregation is now illegal in the United States. But black Americans still have a long way to go before they can say they have reached the 'bright daylight of peace and brotherhood' for which Martin Luther King fought so hard.

Dates

1929 born in Atlanta, Georgia
1948 travels to Boston to study to be a Baptist minister
1954 returns to the South, to Montgomery, Alabama
1956 leads Montgomery bus boycott
1960 joins lunch counter sit-ins and 'Freedom Riders'
1963 organizes non-violent demonstrations in Birmingham, Alabama; leads a huge march to Washington
1964 awarded the Nobel Peace Prize.
1968 assassinated in Memphis, Tennessee

Martin Luther King believed passionately in equal rights and was willing to die for his beliefs.

The *Dalai Lama*

Patient worker for world peace

At the age of five years, Tenzin Gyatso became the fourteenth Dalai Lama, the leader of the Tibetan people. He was forced to leave Tibet in 1959, after the Chinese invaded his country. Now he lives with his followers in northern India and campaigns for freedom for Tibet and for world peace.

When the thirteenth Dalai Lama, the spiritual leader of Tibet, died in 1933, he left some clues for his followers to help them recognize his successor. In 1937, the faithful Buddhist monks found the person they were looking for in a tiny village in north-eastern Tibet. He was a two-year-old boy named Tenzin Gyatso.

The Dalai Lama heads the Tibetan government in exile from his office in Northern India.

Before the Chinese invaded Tibet in 1959, the Dalai Lama ruled his country from the Potala Palace in Lhasa, the capital of Tibet.

The monks took Tenzin Gyatso and his elder brother to live in a monastery at Lhasa, the capital of Tibet. There they educated the child for his future career as Tibet's Dalai Lama. The little boy was enthroned as the Dalai Lama when he was only five years old. Even at that young age, he seemed to understand the important role he was to play in the political and spiritual life of his country.

Tibetan monks listen to a talk by the Dalai Lama in India in 1970.

The Dalai Lama travels all over the world, calling for peace. Here he greets visitors at his home in India.

The young Dalai Lama had an amazing ability to learn and understand Buddhist teachings. He also enjoyed studying English and geography and liked to take things apart and put them together again. As an adult he has proved to be a good and strong leader for his people in times of trouble.

Tibet has been invaded by its Chinese neighbours many times during its long history. At last, in 1912, all the Chinese were thrown out of Tibet and Tibetan independence from China was declared. But in 1950 the Chinese invaded again. The Dalai Lama tried to work with the Chinese to bring peace to his country. He appealed to the United Nations for help, but because Tibet was not a member of the United Nations, and few people knew anything about the country, the appeal was ignored. Finally, in 1959 he was forced to leave Tibet and set up a government in exile in northern India. Many Tibetans followed him to set up a new life in India around their leader.

The Dalai Lama still cannot return to Tibet, which continues to be ruled by China, but he has never stopped trying to find a peaceful solution to his country's tragedy. He has become a respected world leader, travelling to many countries urging compassion and peace for all. Although many people choose to ignore what has happened in Tibet, few can ignore the work of the Dalai Lama. In 1989 he was awarded the Nobel Peace Prize. He believes that everyone must work together to make a better world; 'Whenever I meet a "foreigner" I always feel I am meeting another member of the human family,' he says.

Dates

1935 born Tenzin Gyatso in a village in north-east Tibet
1937 recognized as the Dalai Lama by Buddhist monks
1940 enthroned as the fourteenth Dalai Lama
1950 The Chinese invade Tibet
1959 The Dalai Lama leaves Tibet with followers
1960 sets up a government in exile in northern India
1967 travels abroad to tell the world about Tibet and to preach for peace
1989 awarded the Nobel Peace Prize

In 1989 the Dalai Lama won the Nobel Peace Prize for his work to make a better and more peaceful world for everyone.

Chico *Mendes*

Fighting to save the rainforest

Chico Mendes worked as a rubber tapper in the Brazilian rainforest. He saw how business people were making a lot of money from cutting down huge areas of the forest and he fought to save it. He died because of his efforts to protect the rainforest and to conserve its valuable products. Nowadays, many people are following his ideas and are trying to save the rainforest from being cut down.

Chico Mendes grew up in the rainforest of Brazil. He fought to prevent the destruction of the forest by timber companies, cattle ranchers, and other people anxious to make money from cutting down the trees.

Francisco Alves Mendes Filho Mendes, known to everyone as Chico, was born on 15 December 1944. His parents lived near the town of Xapuri, in the south-western corner of the Amazon rainforest in Brazil. His family were very poor. They had moved from north-eastern Brazil to the rainforest, hoping to make a living by tapping the sap from the rubber trees growing there.

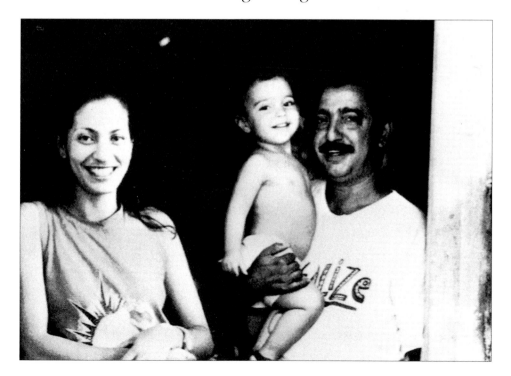

A photograph of Chico Mendes and his family, taken shortly before his murder in 1988.

Chico began working on the rubber plantations when he was just nine years old. There were no schools in the rainforest but he was taught to read by an escaped prisoner who also encouraged the young boy to think about politics.

For many years huge areas of the Amazon rainforest have been destroyed to make way for agricultural land for farmers and cattle ranchers. Trees are also cut down for timber and road-building. Chico Mendes joined with other local people to form the Xapuri Rural Workers Union. They organized a protest against the ranchers who were clearing the forest for grazing for their animals. To try to keep the ranchers out of the rainforest, the union members would gather together in large groups to block areas of forest which were about to be cleared. In this way they saved thousands of hectares from destruction.

Chico Mendes proposed the idea of setting up areas of forest where logging and clearing is banned, but collecting rubber, fruit and other forest products would be allowed. He believed that if this happened, people living in the rainforest would work to protect it, because if they harvested its products wisely, the forest would provide them with a living.

In 1985 Mendes joined with other rubber tappers to form the National Rubber Tappers Council. The Council agreed that the rainforest should be conserved and used for its many valuable and useful products, rather than simply fencing it off as a nature reserve, or even worse, destroying it to provide land for the ranchers.

Mendes travelled to the United States to explain these ideas to international organizations, some of which were themselves involved with the companies cutting down the trees. This visit brought his name to world attention. Environmentalists were becoming increasingly concerned about the devastating effects of rainforest destruction. In addition to the cutting down of trees, huge numbers of plants and animals are being destroyed and the way of life of the rainforest people is disappearing.

Mendes' ideas greatly angered the cattle ranchers. He knew that his life was in danger every time he spoke out for the protection of the rainforest, but he was determined to make his voice heard. A few days before Christmas 1988, Chico Mendes was murdered outside his home in Brazil.

Just before Mendes' death, the Brazilian government took up his ideas and set up the first extractive reserve in the rainforest (an area where logging and clearing is banned.) Since 1988 many environmental groups and others have collected money to set up other such reserves.

Dates

1944 born near Xapuri in Brazil
1953 begins working on rubber plantations
1960 helps to form the Xapuri Rural Workers Union
1985 travels to the United States to discuss his ideas for saving the rainforest
1988 murdered outside his home

(right) The sad reality of rainforest trees that have been burnt and then cut down and cleared.

(left) The Amazon rainforest provides a rich environment for millions of plants and animals.

Aung San Suu Kyi

'A bright collection of strange victories'

Aung San Suu Kyi (known as Suu) was born in Burma. She left the country when she was two years old. After many years living in Britain and other countries, she returned to Burma to look after her sick mother. Burma was now ruled by army generals. She led the people in an election to form a free government, but the army rulers arrested her and kept her a prisoner in her house. She has been cut off from the outside world for more that three years

Although she has been held under house arrest in Burma since 1989, Aung San Suu Kyi (pronounced awng sahn soo chee) is still looked on by the Burmese as their leader in

Aung San Suu Kyi is a determined fighter for democracy in Burma. She is seen here before her arrest, speaking to supporters.

the democratic struggle to free Burma from the harsh rule of a military government. She is isolated from the outside world, but her struggle to bring democracy to Burma is an inspiration to all who care about human rights.

When his daughter was born on 19 June 1945, U Aung San, Burma's national hero and leader in the struggle for independence from Britain, must have guessed what an amazing woman she would become. He chose to name her Aung San Suu Kyi, which means (in English) 'a bright collection of strange victories'.

When Suu was only two years old, her father was assassinated. When she was fifteen she left Burma to study abroad. She received a degree from Oxford University, then lived in America and Bhutan before returning to Britain in 1974 with her British husband, Dr. Michael Aris. Although she lived and studied abroad, Suu always believed that her education was an important preparation for serving her own country.

Burma, officially called Mynanmar, is the westernmost country on the Indochina peninsula in Southeast Asia. In ancient times it was cut off from the outside world by its rugged mountains. Burma gained independence from Britain in 1947, but is now isolated once again by the harsh rule of its government. After an army take-over in 1988 the leaders set up a military council to rule Burma. The rulers promised to

Soldiers prepare to attack the troops of the Burmese military government in the struggle for democracy in Burma.

43

hand over power to a civilian government after holding elections, and they promised that opposing political parties would be allowed to campaign.

Suu returned to Burma in 1988 to look after her sick mother. When she arrived the nation was in turmoil, with many people demonstrating for political and economic change. Suu became a leader in the struggle for democracy and she formed a political party, the National League for Democracy. In July 1989, the military authorities placed her under house arrest. Although she could not speak directly to the Burmese people, when free elections were held in May 1990, Aung San Suu Kyi and her party won most of the votes.

Although held under house arrest since 1989, Suu continues her struggle, using non-violent methods of protest to bring about democracy in her country.

Aung San Suu Kyi won the Nobel Peace Prize in 1991, but she is still imprisoned under house arrest. Supporters around the world pray for her release.

But victory for the National League for Democracy has not yet brought democracy to Burma. Since the elections, the military authorities have forced the National League for Democracy to dismiss Suu as their leader. For nearly three years she was kept in total isolation in her own house. In May 1992 she was finally allowed visits from her husband and children. The authorities are still trying to persuade her to go into exile.

In spite of the hardships, Suu remains committed to the use of non-violent and democratic means to bring about a Burmese society that is free from fear. Although she cannot speak out directly, her ideals have inspired many people all over the world. She has received many prizes in recognition of her work, including the Nobel Peace Prize in 1991. She writes; 'Even under the most crushing state machinery, courage rises up again and again, for fear is not the natural state of a civilized people.'

Dates

1945 born in Burma
1947 her father, U Aung San, is assassinated
1960 travels abroad to study
1967 received degree from Oxford University
1974 settles in Britain with her English husband
1988 returns to Burma to care for her sick mother; forms the National League for Democracy
1989 placed under house arrest
1990 National League for Democracy wins elections
1991 awarded the Nobel Peace Prize

Glossary

Abolitionists   People who worked to end the slave trade.

African National Congress   An African nationalist movement that works to oppose apartheid.

Anti-apartheid   To be against the policy of apartheid (see below).

Apartheid   Formerly official government policy in South Africa to keep people of different races apart.

Assassination   Violent murder, usually for political reasons.

American Civil War   A war fought between the Southern and Northern states of the United States between 1861-65.

Baptist Church   A branch of the Protestant Christian Church.

Bhutan   A kingdom in central Asia.

Boycott   To refuse to have dealings with something or someone.

Buddhist   Relating to the religion taught by the Buddha.

Civil rights   The personal right of individuals.

Colonies   Countries settled and governed by another ruling country.

Conserve   To keep or protect from harm.

Consul-general   A government official in a foreign country.

Democracy   A form of government whose members have been freely elected.

Environment   The surroundings as they affect living things.

Environmentalists   People who are concerned with the living conditions of plants and animals.

Exile   Forced to live outside one's own country.

Fast   To go without food.

General strike   When all the workers in a country stop work as a protest.

Grazing   Vegetation that is grown for animals to eat.

Hindu   A follower of the religion of Hinduism.

House arrest   To be imprisoned in one's own home.

Human rights   The rights of individuals to liberty, justice etc.

Hygiene   The study of the rules of health and cleanliness.

Lepers   People with a serious skin disease called leprosy.

Mission   The building or centre where missionaries carry out medical or other charitable work.

Missionary   A member of a group of people sent out to do religious and social work.

Muslim   A follower of the religion of Islam.

Nobel Peace Prize   A prize awarded each year for outstanding achievements for world peace.

Passive resistance   A non-violent form of protest when large numbers of people refuse to obey unjust laws and calmly take punishment.

Plantation Large estates where crops such as rice, cotton and tobacco are grown.

Satyagraha Gandhi's term for the truth force, which inspired his ideals of non-violent protest.

Second-class citizen A person whose rights and opportunities are treated as less important those of other people.

Segregation A system of laws and customs which aim to separate white people from black people.

Slavery A system whereby people are owned and forced to work by others.

Spiritual Relating to religion.

Treason A crime that involves betraying one's country.

United Nations An international organization of independent countries that was formed to promote peace and security.

Vows Solemn promises to God.

Books to read and further information

Aaseng, Nathan *The Peace Seekers - The Nobel Peace Prize* (Lerner, 1988)
Banks, Martin *Conserving the Rainforests* (Wayland, 1990)
Brown, Pam *Florence Nightingale* (Exley Publications, 1988)
Clucas, Joan Graff *Mother Teresa* (Harrap, 1990)
Gibb, Christopher *Dalai Lama* (Exley Publications, 1990)
Hunter, Nigel *Twenty Campaigners for Change* (Wayland, 1987)
Killingray, David *The Transatlantic Slave Trade* (Batsford, 1987)
McKissack, P.C. & F. *Frederick Douglass* (Enslow Publishers, 1991)
Nicolson, Mike *Mahatma Gandhi* (Exley, 1987)
Pollard, Michael *People who Care* by Michael Pollard (Heinemann, 1991))
Pollard, Michael *Maria Montessori* (Exley, Publications, 1987)
Prosser, Robert *Disappearing Rainforest* (Dryad Press, 1987)
Richardson, Nigel *Martin Luther King* (Evan Brothers, 1992)
Tames, Richard *Nelson Mandela* (Franklin Watts, 1991)

Useful addresses

Greenpeace (UK)
30-31 Islington Green
London EC1

Greenpeace (Canada)
2623 West 4th Avenue
Vancouver BCV6K 1p8

Greenpeace (Australia)
3l0 Angas Street
Adelaide 5000

Amnesty International (British Section)
99-119 Rosebery Avenue
London EC1R 4RE

Index

abolitionists 6
African National
  Congress 25, 26, 27, 28
Amazon rainforest 38
  destruction of 39, 41
American Civil War 6, 7
anti-apartheid campaign 27,
  28
apartheid laws 26
Aung San Suu Kyi 42-5
  studies in Britain and USA 43
  returns to Burma 44
  forms National League of
    Democracy 44
  placed under house arrest 44
  elections held 44
  dismissed as political
    leader 45
  awarded Nobel Peace
    Prize 45

Buddhist religion 34
Burma 42, 43

Calcutta 20
Catholic Church 22
civil rights movement 32
Dalai Lama 34-7
  discovered by monks 34
  enthroned as Dalai Lama 35
  China invades Tibet 36
  Dalai Lama appeals to United
    Nations 36
  leaves Tibet to live in exile 37
  travels and urges peace
    worldwide 37
  awarded Nobel Peace
    Prize 37
democracy 42, 45
Douglass, Frederick 4-7
  escapes from slavery 6
  writes book about his life as a
    slave 6
  lectures in Europe 7
  becomes advisor to President
    Lincoln 7

environmentalists 41
extractive reserves 41

Freedom Riders 36

Gandhi, Mohandas 12-15
  studies law in England 13
  works in South Africa 13
  campaigns for Indian rights in
    South Africa 13
  his principle of non-violent
    protest 13, 33
  returns to India 14
  organizes one-day strike 14
  prison sentence 14, 15
  protests against British
    rule 14
  fasts 15
  assassinated 15

hospitals 9
human rights 4

India, British rule in 12, 13, 14
Indian independence 15

King, Martin Luther 29-33
  studies to become a
    minister 30
  organizes bus boycott 31
  organizes non-violent
    protests 32
  leads civil rights march to
    Washington 32
  awarded Nobel Peace
    Prize 33
  assassinated 33
Klerk, F.W. de 28

Mandela, Nelson 25-28
  studies law 26
  joins ANC 26
  charged with treason 27
  forbidden to attend meetings
    or leave Johannesburg 27
  imprisoned 28
  President of ANC 28
Mendes, Chico 38-41
  works on rubber
    plantation 39
  joins Xapuri Rural Workers
    Union 39

proposes idea of extractive
  reserves 39
helps form National Rubber
  Tappers Council 41
travels to USA 41
murdered 41
Missionaries of Charity 22, 23,
  24
Montessori, Maria
  gains medical degree 16
  founds school for children with
    learning problems 17
  sets up *Casa dei Bambini* in
    Rome 17
  sets up training schools 18
  Montessori teaching
    method 18, 19
Mother Teresa 20-24
  becomes a nun 21
  teaches in Calcutta 21
  founds Missionaries of
    Charity 22
  awarded Nobel Peace
    Prize 24
Mynanmar, see Burma

Nightingale, Florence 8-11
  studies nursing 9
  goes to Crimean War to care
    for wounded soldiers 9
  returns a heroine 20
  sets up Nightingale School for
    Nurses 10, 11
  awarded Order of Merit 11

Satyagraha 13
segregation laws 30

Tibet 34
  Chinese invasion of 36

'underground railroad' 6